T0068243

—— Trevor Wye ——

——FLUTE CLASS——

A GROUP TEACHING BOOK
FOR STUDENTS AND TEACHERS

Piano accompaniments by Robert Scott

Order No: NOV 120738

NOVELLO PUBLISHING LIMITED

CROSSOVERS

(page 8)

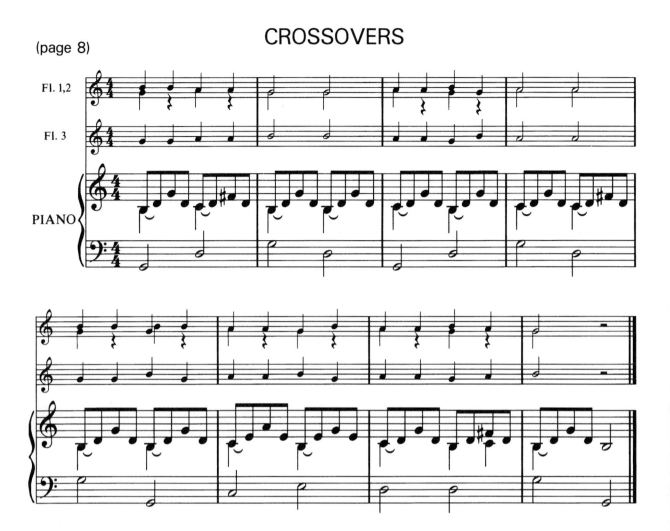

(page 9)

AIR DE BUFFONS

16th century

1

(page 12)

WALTZ

(page 14)

DANCE

SUSATO

(page 18)

THE MAIDEN

Fl. 1,2

(page 18)

MELODY

LULLY

Fl. 1,2

AIR DE BUFFONS

16th century

GERMAN DANCE

M. FRANCK

MAYPOLE DANCE

TRADITIONAL

CAN-CAN

OFFENBACH

SAD WALTZ

18th century

(page 33)

DANCE

HAUPTMANN

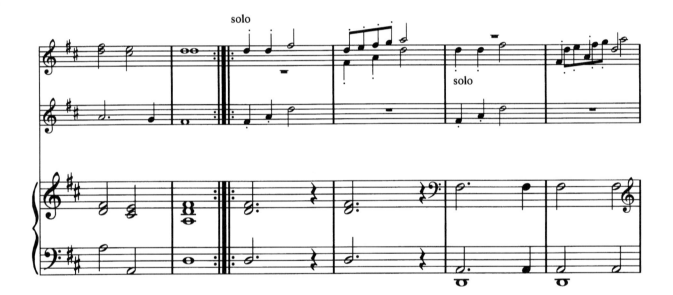

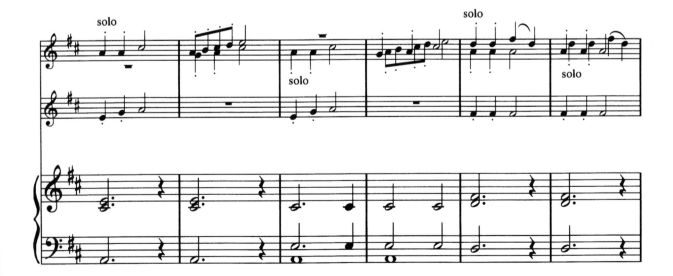

(page 34)

THE STREETS OF LAREDO

TRADITIONAL

Moderato

Fl. 1,2

9

WALTZ

SCHUBERT

Tempo di valse

FINE

D.C. al Fine

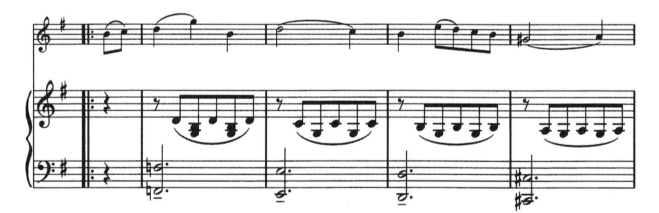

(page 42)

TAMBOURIN

RAMEAU

SOUVENIR DE GAND

SEGHERS

(page 52)

THE AQUARIUM

SAINT SAËNS

Fl. 1,2

Fl. 3

13

WALTZ

SCHUBERT

THE HARVESTERS

COUPERIN

Allegretto con spirito

Fl. 1

FL. 2,3

FINE

FINE

D.C. al Fine

D.C. al Fine

MANGO WALK

TRADITONAL

(page 83)

DANCE

PRAETORIUS

Giocoso

17

(page 77)

GOD REST YE MERRY, GENTLEMEN

TRADITIONAL